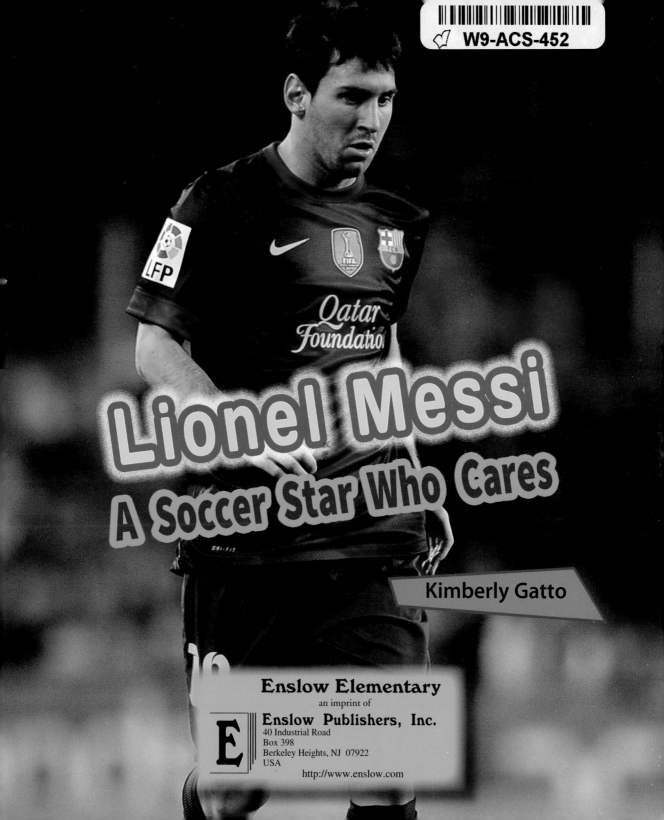

Lionel Messi
A Soccer Star Who Cares

Kimberly Gatto

Enslow Elementary
an imprint of
Enslow Publishers, Inc.
40 Industrial Road
Box 398
Berkeley Heights, NJ 07922
USA

http://www.enslow.com

Enslow Elementary, an imprint of Enslow Publishers, Inc.

Enslow Elementary® is a registered trademark of Enslow Publishers, Inc.

Library of Congress Cataloging-in-Publication Data

Gatto, Kimberly.
  Lionel Messi : a soccer star who cares / Kimberly Gatto.
      p. cm. — (Sports stars who care)
   Includes bibliographical references and index.
   Summary: "Learn about international soccer star, Lionel Messi, and all that he has had to overcome to be where he is now. This sports biography goes into his successes, his struggles, and how he has proven that he is a sports star who cares"—Provided by publisher.
   ISBN 978-0-7660-4299-5
   1. Messi, Lionel, 1987—Juvenile literature. 2. Soccer players—Argentina—Biography—Juvenile literatrue.
I. Title.
   GV942.7.M398G38 2013
   796.334092—dc23
   [B]   2012039665

Future editions:
Paperback ISBN: 978-1-4644-0543-3   EPUB ISBN: 978-1-4645-1277-3
Single-User PDF ISBN: 978-1-4646-1277-0   Multi-User PDF: 978-0-7660-5909-2

Printed in the United States of America

052014 Lake Book Manufacturing, Inc., Melrose Park, IL

10 9 8 7 6 5 4 3

To Our Readers: We have done our best to make sure all Internet addresses in this book were active and appropriate when we went to press. However, the author and the Publisher have no control over, and assume no liability for, the material available on those Internet sites or on other Web sites they may link to. Any comments or suggestions can be sent by e-mail to comments@enslow.com or to the address on the back cover.

♻ Enslow Publishers, Inc., is committed to printing our books on recycled paper. The paper in every book contains 10% to 30% post-consumer waste (PCW). The cover board on the outside of each book contains 100% PCW. Our goal is to do our part to help young people and the environment too!

Photo Credits: AP Images/Armando Franca, pp. 28, 40; AP Images/Daisuke Tomita/The Yomiuri Shimbun, p. 16; AP Images/Daniel Ochoa De Olza, p. 4; AP Images/Fernando Vergara, p. 26; AP Images/Francisco Seco, p. 15; AP Images/Israel Leal, p. 35; AP Images/Juan Jose Garcia, p. 8; AP Images/Keystone/Walter Bieri, p. 44; AP Images/Manu Fernandez, pp. 1, 21, 31, 37, 38; AP Images/Michael Probst, p. 32; AP Images/Pavel Rahman, p. 23; AP Images/Ricardo Mazalan, p. 13; AP Images/Roberto Candia, p. 19; AP Images/Shuji Kajiyama, p. 11; AP Images/Victor R. Caivano, p. 10.

Cover Photo: AP Images/Manu Fernandez

Contents

Lionel ("Leo") Messi is often called a "giant" on the soccer field. That is because he makes a huge difference to his team. But Leo is not a tall man. He stands 5 feet, 6-and-a-half inches. Leo plays for the La Liga club FC Barcelona in Spain. He is also the captain of the Argentine national team. Argentina is a country in South America.

Many fans call Leo by his nickname, "La Pulga." That means "the flea" in Spanish. Like a flea, Leo is small and quick. He is able to squeeze into tight places. He can wriggle by the strongest defenders. Leo is not afraid of the bigger players. In fact, he always keeps them guessing! Leo's teammate Gerard Piqué once said, "Leo simply goes one way with his body and another with the ball. You have to either guess right or foul him."

Leo Messi is a versatile player. He can play any of the forward positions. Forwards are sometimes called "strikers." They play nearest to the opposing team's goal. Forwards are usually responsible for scoring goals. Leo is sometimes called a "ghost center forward." Like a ghost, he "floats" around rather than staying in one position. He can also play the "false nine" spot. The false nine plays deep in the midfield. This makes it difficult for the opposing center backs. If they stay with him, there is an open space for other players to break through. But if they do not cover him, he may dribble or pick out a pass.

Leo is one of the greatest soccer players in the world. He has already been named Player of the Year four times. Many people believe he is one of best players in the history of soccer. Arsène Wenger, coach of the Arsenal team in England, said, "(Messi) is (like) a PlayStation. Once he's on the run, (he) is unstoppable. He is the best player in the world by some distance."

Lionel Andrés Messi was born on June 24, 1987 in Rosario, Argentina. He was the third child born to Jorge and Celia Messi. Leo has two older brothers, Rodrigo and Matías. He also has a younger sister, María Sol. Leo's parents worked hard to support their family. Jorge worked at a metals

Chapter 1

Early Years

company. Celia helped out by working as a house cleaner.

Soccer has always been a popular sport in Argentina. It was also a favorite pastime in the Messi family. Rodrigo and Matías played for the local club, Grandioli. Rodrigo played as a center forward. Matías was a defender.

Messi was honored alongside his mother (right) by Mayor Mónica Fein as Honorary Citizen of his hometown of Rosario, Argentina.

At first, Leo seemed more interested in playing with marbles than soccer balls. That changed when he was only three years old. While watching his brothers play, Leo decided to join in. Rodrigo and Matías were impressed. Leo was fast and could kick the ball hard. Soon he became a part of the neighborhood matches.

One day, Leo's grandmother spoke with Ricardo Aparicio, Grandioli's soccer coach. Aparicio needed another boy for his team. Leo's grandmother told Aparicio how well Leo could play. But the coach was not sure if Leo was ready to join the team. Leo was very small for his age. At age five, he was also a year younger than the other boys. Aparicio worried that Leo might get hurt.

Leo's family convinced Aparicio to watch the little boy play. Aparicio was amazed. He agreed that Leo could join the team. Aparicio later said, "The second (the ball) came to his left foot, he latched onto it, and he went past one guy, then another and another." There was no question that Leo belonged on the team.

Messi mainly plays for FC Barcelona, but he also gets to play for Argentina, his home country.

Messi dribbles past a defender from Brazil's Santos FC. Many believed Messi was too small to play soccer at an elite level. Then they watched him fly by defenders with moves like this.

That season, Leo helped his team win many games. They won both the local friendlies and the bigger league tournaments. The next year, Grandioli won the year-end championship. At six years old, The Flea was on his way to soccer stardom.

By the time he was seven years old, Leo Messi was making a name for himself. People talked about the little boy who could score many goals. Soon, the coach of a club called Newell's Old Boys heard about Leo. The club had one of the best boys' soccer teams in all of Argentina. Their team, called the "Lepers," had won many national championships. Even the superstar Diego Maradona

Chapter 2

A Step Up

had once played for the Lepers. At one time, Maradona was the greatest soccer player in the world. In 1986, he led Argentina to victory in the World Cup.

Newell's Old Boys was well known to the Messi family. Jorge had played there when he was a boy.

Argentina head coach Diego Maradona (left) mentors Messi. Maradona was once viewed as the best soccer player alive.

Rodrigo and Matías followed. One day, the boys' coach invited Leo to join his brothers at practice. The coach wanted to see for himself if Leo was that good. Over the next month, Leo was allowed to play in many of the team's matches. Sometimes he played as a forward. Other times he was asked to defend. Leo handled all these tests like a pro. Soon he became an official member of the team.

Leo played in many tournaments with the Lepers. To get himself ready for matches, he often did tricks with the ball. Leo especially liked to play "keepy uppy." This is a type of juggling the soccer ball, with the object being to not let it reach the ground. Other players enjoyed watching Leo balance the ball with his feet and legs. Soon the managers asked Leo if he would perform these tricks for the crowds. Even though he was shy, Leo agreed. People cheered in the stands as Leo juggled during halftime breaks.

Playing "keepy uppy" was just one way in which Leo worked to improve his skills. He always tried to make himself better. Leo also worked hard in school. Sometimes it was not easy. Leo found reading and

Leo still plays "keepy uppy" before each match to better perfect his control of the ball.

Messi is about to lob the ball over the head of Santos FC goalie Rafael Cabral. FC Barcelona beat Santos FC to win the 2011 FIFA Club World Cup.

writing difficult. His favorite subjects were art and gym. He also did not like to talk in front of class. But Leo's parents had taught him to always try his best. They also taught him to respect others. Leo never bragged about how many goals he scored or how many trophies he had. Because of this, Leo had many friends in school and on the field.

Besides his positive attitude, Leo had a strong will to win. During one game, Leo was not feeling well. As he sat on the bench, the team struggled. The team was losing 1–0 with five minutes left. Even though he was not feeling 100%, Leo returned to the game. As he ran towards the field, the coach yelled to him, "Win me the match!"

Leo did just that. He netted two goals, and the Lepers won the game. By now, Leo was scoring almost 100 goals each season. Leo's coach, Ernesto Vecchio, was not surprised. "(Leo) was something special," he said. "He did not need to be taught a thing."

At the age of eleven, Leo stood only four-feet, four-inches tall. He was much smaller than other boys his age. Leo's parents began to worry that something was wrong. They took him to a doctor for tests. Jorge and Celia hoped the doctor could find out why Leo was not growing.

The doctor found that Leo's body was not making enough

Chapter 3

Barcelona

Messi and Argentina teammate Oscar Ustari have fun before their match in the 2006 World Cup.

growth hormone. Without this chemical, the body does not grow. Fortunately this could be treated with medicine. Leo would have to get a daily shot in his arm for the next several years. Without the treatment, Leo would not grow much more than a few more inches.

But the medicine was very expensive. It could cost up to $1,000 every month. At first, the family's insurance paid for some of the cost. Soon, however, the insurance ran out. The Messis did not have the money to pay for Leo's medicine.

Luckily, there was someone who could afford it. The owners of the FC Barcelona soccer team in Spain had heard about Leo's talent. They wanted Leo to try out for their team. The director of the team, Carles Rexach, invited Leo's dad to bring him to Barcelona. Leo would play in a series of practice matches. If they chose Leo for the team, the club would pay for his medicine.

Leo and his father made the trip to Barcelona. Rexach placed Leo in a scrimmage, where he scored five goals. Afterward, Rexach took Leo and his dad aside. He asked if Leo wanted to join FC Barcelona.

The club would pay for all of Leo's medication. They would also pay for the family to move to Spain.

Rexach wanted Leo to sign a contract right away. Rexach did not want to take a chance that Leo would play for a different team. But Rexach did not have any paper on hand. So he quickly grabbed a paper napkin instead. First, Rexach signed the napkin. Then he had Leo and his dad sign it. The deal was done. It may have

Messi signed his first contract at the age of thirteen on a napkin.

been the first sports contract that was written on a napkin!

Back at home, the Messi family knew that it would be difficult to leave Argentina. They would miss their friends and relatives. But everyone wanted to do what was best for Leo. Jorge and Celia sat around the dinner table and asked the children what they thought about moving. Rodrigo, Matías, and María Sol all had the same answer. They wanted to move to Spain so that Leo would receive his medication.

That year, the Messis packed up and moved to Barcelona. The club found an apartment for the family. Jorge got a new job, and the children started school. And Leo began his daily medication. Soon, he began growing. The medication was working.

At Barcelona, Leo was placed on a team for boys under fourteen years of age. The team had a strict workout schedule. Leo and his teammates practiced hard. Each day they trained with the ball. They learned different moves, including kicking and running. Leo later said, "I hardly even took a step running without a ball at my feet."

After Lionel signed with Barcelona, there was rarely a moment when he did not have a soccer ball at his feet.

Once again, Leo's hard work paid off. He soon became the star of the team. Leo quickly moved up through the club ranks. He was chosen for the club's top team, the "A" team, when he was only sixteen years old. Around this time, Leo became the star of a local newspaper article. The reporter wrote, "Despite his height, (Messi) can go past one, past two, beat all the defenders and score goals. But above all, he has fun with the ball."

Leo began the 2004 season for Barcelona as a reserve player. He played when the starters were out with injuries. Leo made the most of his time on the field by running fast and scoring goals. Soon he was asked to play in more games.

By the time he was eighteen, Leo had begun setting records. On May 1, 2005, Leo became the youngest player ever to score a league goal

Chapter 4

Pro Player

Pablo Zabaleta embraces Messi after Leo's goal during the 2005 South America Under-20 championships.

for FC Barcelona. That season he also led Argentina to victory in the FIFA Under-20 World Cup. In the final, he scored both of Argentina's goals on penalty shots. Leo earned awards for being both the top scorer and the top player on his team.

Leo soon became a fan favorite. The crowds often stood on their feet and cheered for him. Many held signs that said, "Go Messi!" Leo played very well with Ronaldinho, who was Barcelona's main star at that time. Together with Ronaldinho, Leo handled the toughest opponents with ease.

Leo also continued to set new records. In 2006, he became the youngest player to appear in a World Cup for Argentina. He also was the youngest Argentine player ever to score a World Cup goal. Leo finished the season with 14 goals. People soon began to compare him to the great Diego Maradona. Some fans called him "Messidona," a nickname created from "Messi" and "Maradona."

With each year, Leo seemed to get better and better. In 2008, he became Barcelona's superstar when Ronaldinho left the team. Leo switched his No. 19 for

Ronaldinho's No. 10 jersey. Number 10 is usually worn by the best player on a team.

In the summer of 2008, Messi was excited to represent Argentina at the Beijing Olympics. He

Against Ivory Coast in the 2008 Olympics, Messi was at his best. Argentina went on to win the gold medal.

played like a true superstar. In the final versus Nigeria, Leo made the setup for the only goal of the game. Leo and team Argentina won the gold medal.

Afterwards, reporters asked Leo for his favorite Olympic memory. Leo described having lunch with basketball star Kobe Bryant. The two stars spoke in Spanish. Bryant told Leo that he is a huge fan of soccer. He told Leo how much he enjoyed watching him play. Before he left the table, Bryant said, "Messi—you're the best!"

Leo proved that Bryant was right. In the 2009–10 season, Lionel set several more records for Barcelona. During one week, he netted eight goals. Leo then became the first player in Barcelona's history to score back-to-back hat tricks in league games. The fans were going crazy over him. In 2010 a Spanish bakery even made a life-size statue of Leo—out of chocolate!

Chapter 5

The Best

Messi celebrates after scoring a goal against archrival Real Madrid.

Messi has won the Ballon d'Or four times as the world's best player.

The following season, Leo set a Spanish record by scoring 53 official goals. In 2011, he won the Ballon d'Or ("Golden Ball") award as the best player in the sport. It was the third time Leo was given this honor.

Leo continued his winning ways in the 2011–12 season. That year, Leo surpassed 232 goals to become Barcelona's top goal scorer of all time. That same week, he thrilled the fans when he scored five goals in a single game. He set the all-time record for goals in a La Liga season. His tally of 91 goals in a calendar year is also unmatched.

Messi's worldwide stardom continued to grow. In 2012 he appeared in ads for both Pepsi and Lays potato chips. By now, Leo was regarded as the top soccer player in the world. He won his fourth Ballon d'Or. He was the first player to win the award four times. Leo's teammate, Deco, summed it up when he said, "There's no other like Leo."

Like most sports stars, Leo Messi likes to win. But he also knows that winning is not everything. Leo knows that a true champion does not just run fast or score goals. A true champion gives to others.

When he is not playing soccer, Leo spends much of his time helping children. In 2007, he established the Leo Messi Foundation.

Chapter 6

Making A Difference

Messi organizes friendly soccer matches to raise money for his charity, the Leo Messi Foundation.

The foundation builds parks and schools in poor areas. It also provides treatment for children who are sick. The motto of the foundation is "Choose to Believe." That is because Leo wants to give people hope.

Leo also is a member of UNICEF, a charity that helps children throughout the world. In 2010, Leo was named goodwill ambassador for UNICEF. In this role, he visits with people who need help. For example, in 2010, Leo visited parts of Haiti that had been hit by an earthquake. Leo worked on a plan to build new shelters for people who had lost their homes. He also taped a commercial and appears in magazine ads for UNICEF.

Leo enjoys meeting his young fans. In 2007, he heard about a boy named Soufian who lives in Africa. Soufian had lost both of his legs to an illness. Even without legs, Soufian loved to play soccer. Leo met with Soufian and they played a friendly game. Leo then had a special surprise for Soufian. In his next game, he would score his first goal for him. To let Soufian know that the goal was for him, Leo would slap his hands against his legs.

Messi is not only the Goodwill Ambassador for UNICEF. He enjoys making appearances for the group because he loves being around children.

Messi and the rest of FC Barcelona give gifts to children in a Barcelona hospital every year around Christmas.

Leo kept his promise. In his next game, against Osasuna, Leo slapped his legs after scoring the first goal. It was a huge thrill for Soufian, who was watching the game. Leo went on to score two more goals, earning a hat trick for that game. After the game, one of the sportscasters shouted, "Messi is huge, Messi is huge!"

In 2012, Leo found out about another young fan who needed help. Waleed, a boy from Morocco, suffers from a growth hormone problem. Leo sent a letter to Waleed and his family. In the letter, he told Waleed's family that he would pay for all of the boy's medicine!

Leo enjoys meeting his young fans. In between games, he often visits sick kids in hospitals. He spends time chatting with them and often brings them gifts. After one visit, Leo said, "They smile and for them it is a special joy. I get excited every day that a child smiles when he thinks that there is hope, when I see him happy."

Leo hopes to help many more children through his foundation in the years to come. "Being a bit

Messi fights for the ball with Jardel Vieira of Benfica.

famous now gives me the opportunity to help people who really need it, particularly children," he said. Leo Messi is truly a soccer star who cares!

Career Statistics

Year	Team	Competition	Games Started	Used as Sub	Goals	Shots	Assists	Fouls Suffered
2004-05	Barcelona	UCL	1	0	0	0	0	0
2004-05	Barcelona	La Liga	0	7	1	0	0	0
2005-06	Barcelona	La Liga	11	6	6	32	0	0
2005-06	Barcelona	UCL	4	2	1	20	1	0
2006-07	Barcelona	UCL	4	1	1	7	0	0
2006-07	Barcelona	La Liga	23	3	14	46	2	0
2006-07	Argentina	WC	1	2	1	3	1	0
2006-07	Argentina	Int	3	0	1	0	0	0
2006-07	Barcelona	Esp Cup	2	0	2	0	0	0
2006-07	Barcelona	Super C	1	0	0	0	0	0
2007-08	Barcelona	Esp Cup	1	0	0	0	0	0
2007-08	Barcelona	La Liga	23	5	10	68	12	72
2007-08	Barcelona	UCL	12	0	8	37	1	31
2007-08	Argentina	WCQ	4	0	2	9	1	12
2008-09	Argentina	WCQ	8	0	2	8	2	33
2008-09	Barcelona	UCL	10	2	9	32	5	25
2008-09	Barcelona	La Liga	27	4	23	114	11	83
2008-09	Argentina	Oly	5	0	2	0	0	0
2008-09	Barcelona	Esp Cup	4	4	6	0	0	0
2009-10	Barcelona	Esp Cup	3	0	1	0	0	0
2009-10	Barcelona	Super C	1	0	0	0	0	0
2009-10	Barcelona	CWC	1	1	2	40	0	6
2009-10	Barcelona	La Liga	30	5	34	163	10	84
2009-10	Barcelona	UCL	11	0	8	52	0	30
2009-10	Argentina	WCQ	10	0	2	15	1	33
2009-10	Argentina	Int	2	0	2	2	0	5

Year	Team	Competition	Games Started	Used as Sub	Goals	Shots	Assists	Fouls Suffered
2010-11	Argentina	Int	3	0	1	7	0	10
2010-11	Barcelona	UCL	11	2	12	69	3	37
2010-11	Barcelona	La Liga	31	2	31	150	18	57
2010-11	Barcelona	Esp Cup	5	2	7	0	0	0
2010-11	Argentina	WC	5	0	0	29	1	15
2011-12	Barcelona	Esp Cup	5	2	3	0	0	0
2011-12	Argentina	Copa Am	4	0	0	6	3	18
2011-12	Barcelona	Sup Cup	2	0	3	7	2	5
2011-12	Barcelona	CWC	2	0	2	3	1	3
2011-12	Barcelona	Super C	1	0	1	0	0	0
2011-12	Barcelona	La Liga	36	1	50	198	15	78
2011-12	Barcelona	UCL	11	0	14	76	5	28
2011-12	Argentina	Int	4	0	2	2	0	4
2011-12	Argentina	WCQ	5	0	2	12	1	14
2012-13	Argentina	WCQ	9	0	7	28	2	24
2012-13	Argentina	Int	4	0	7	4	0	1
2012-13	Barcelona	UCL	5	1	5	29	2	11
2012-13	Barcelona	La Liga	17	1	27	95	6	45
2012-13	Barcelona	Sup Cup	2	0	2	8	0	7
2012-13	Barcelona	Esp Cup	1	0	2	0	0	0
Career	Barcelona		298	1	285	1,210	94	602
	Argentina		67	2	31	122	12	173

(Statistics as of January 8, 2013)

43

LIONEL MESSI
c/o FC BARCELONA
Press Office
Avenida Arístes Maillol, s/n
08028 Barcelona, Spain

Barcelona—The second largest city in Spain.

center forward—The player who usually scores goals.

contract—An agreement that is written and enforceable by law.

defender—A player who tries to stop the opposing team from scoring.

dribble—To run and move with the soccer ball at one's feet.

false nine—A forward who plays deep in the midfield to create space for other forwards to run and score.

FIFA—The Fédération Internationale de Football Assocation. This is soccers world governing body.

forward—See striker.

friendlies—Local matches that do not count in a soccer league.

ghost center forward—A forward who does not stay in one position, but floats around the front line.

growth hormone—A substance produced by the body that helps children to grow.

hat trick—A player scoring three goals in a match.

insurance—A practice in which a company pays for medicine for an illness or injury.

keepy uppy—A form of juggling with the soccer ball. In this activity, the player or players try to keep the ball from hitting the ground without using their hands.

Leo Messi Foundation—Foundation started by Messi to young people in at-risk situations.

Morrocco—A country in the northwest corner of Africa very close to Spain.

Olympics—An international athletic event held once every four years. Soccer is part of the Summer Olympics.

reserve player—A member of a team who plays if a starter drops out.

scrimmage—A practice session or informal game.

starter—A player in the starting lineup of a game.

striker—Another word for a forward; a soccer player who plays upfront and tries to score.

UNICEF—The United Nations Children's Fund, formerly known as the United Nations International Children's Emergency Fund. The goal of the fund is to aid children facing poverty and other ills.

World Cup—A soccer tournament held every four years between national soccer teams to determine a world champion.

Read More

Books

Caioli, Luca. *Messi: The Inside Story of the Boy Who Became a Legend*. London: Corinthian Books, 2012.

Hunter, Graham. *Barca: The Making of the Greatest Team in the World*. United Kingdom: BackPage Press Limited, 2012.

Obregón, José María. *Lionel Messi*. New York: PowerKids Press, 2009.

Internet Addresses

Leo Messi Foundation
<http://www.fundacionleomessi.org>

Official FC Barcelona Web Site
<http://www.fcbarcelona.com/>

FIFA Official Site
<http://www.fifa.com/>